# DOWN TO EARTH

## Common Sense Spirituality and Self-Empowerment

by Lynda Lichti

*This book is dedicated to all beings on this planet who are awakened and committed to their spiritual work and their life mission. This book is also dedicated to those who have left their physical vessels and continue their work from the higher dimensions. I AM deeply grateful to all the beings who have assisted me during my journey in this and many other lifetimes.*

*We Are One!*

*~Knowledge is knowing what to say. Wisdom is knowing whether or not to say it~*

*Anonymous*

# CONTENTS

# FOREWORD

## *A New Cycle Has Begun: The Evolutionary Leap In Human Consciousness*

We are living in truly unprecedented times. For those of us who have the life experience of living before the Internet was considered a daily necessity, let alone an extension of ourselves, we know how technology has dramatically changed our world. This has enabled the planet to become a much smaller place with huge potentials; but what about our physcial bodies?

The debates regarding whether or not we have used technology well is still ongoing. However, I would like to shine a light on a more multidimensional perspective and how this affects our physical bodies. This reflects how humans are currently undergoing the leap in evolution with their consciousness and reclaiming personal power that dwarfs the technology currently available to the majority of people on the planet.

There are currently many humans waking up to their true selves. That is a bold statement but I am also part of that community and can speak from my personal experience. I have written previous articles about developing your senses and what that truly means. I now wish to convey a larger point for the entire collective of people who may not understand what is currently happening.

Everything at it's foundation is generally speaking, energy. Most people understand this very basic concept. Instead of trying to explain String Theory and true time, I will simply use my words to paint the picture of what is happening to your bodies at this very moment. I may present some points that challenge your very core belief structures but I ask you to suspend disbeliefs and use your discernment.

The basic concept of energy in the physical world is that all solid matter vibrates at a certain frequency along a spectrum. On one end you have dense matter that vibrates slow. The other end would be invisible to your physical eyes because it would vibrate fast.

When we begin to understand these concepts you can approach healing your physical body with a brand new perspective. The ancient Art of Energy Healing goes back as long as humans have existed. Finally, energy healing is rightfully becoming more mainstream because it works at a fundamental level and has proven to be effective. There are many sources for you to do your own research about energy healing. Most likely, you already have experience or knowledge with some type of energetic healing modality.

There are many new types of healing technologies based on frequency alone.

Not everyone is aware that electronic frequencies have been considered a viable option for treating various diseases including cancer, for a very long time. If this interests you I suggest you research Dr. Royal Rife. The more disclosure we receive *as a collective* the more we can demand these technologies be released. The good news is that times are definitely changing and the technology that can help us *(and not poison us)* is finally going to become mainstream. But it's still a process.

Self-generating BioEnergy is your natural birthright and available to everyone that has a human body. I've been involved in energy healing since 1998 and I've seen a lot happen over the years. The type of frequency a person self generates comes from the portal vortex of energy in the center of your chest also-known-as your heart center; or as a lot of people call it, your heart chakra.

Humans are currently going through a grand

awakening all across the planet. They are becoming more aware of the truth about their multidimensional being. The leap in human consciousness is happening right now as we are in the midst of unprecedented times traversing the river of photonic light through spiraling plasma waves while our physical bodies are also along for this journey.
This light will continue to increase the baseline frequency of not only our planet but our bodies as well. The baseline frequency will continnue to increase until it stablizes for quite some time, to fifth dimensional frequency. This will undoubtely bring up the more dense physical issues in people who are still sleeping, or just hitting the snooze button with their personal awakening to the true state of their multidimensional being.

People tend to cling to things that are familiar. Change is difficult for those who have no concept of living a multidimensional life. Their conditioning has solidified belief structures and it's not easy to let go of core beliefs that were handed to you from childhood. I talk in detail about all of this later in the book.

Self-empowerment is the first step to reclaiming your personal power and is usually triggered by your awakening in the ascension process in most cases.

Some people are waking up fast with no prior

understanding in this particular life or experience, of this ascension process and evolutionary leap in consciousness. There are many beings incarnated as humans who are here to help. One of the main reasons I wrote this book is to help people understand what is happening in a common sense, basic and practical way.

Additionally, I want to help dispel the myths surrounding what the ascension process is all about byt explaing steps you can take for personal power as empowerment for everyone.

The search for your soul continues and as you awaken to your true inner connection to *all that is,* you find your own energy source that is always available. You find that you can make an actual connection to this eternal source and begin to use your senses in a multidimensional way.

Once you discover what you really are you can ignite your gifts enabling you to heal, create, manifest and live an intentional life that is in alignment with your true purpose. You no longer look out into the physical world for information or validation about who you are and why you are here; you walk in your authentic nature with the full capacity of your entire multidimensional self.

I understand self-empowerment is the key to moving forward and this is why I share what I know.

As long as people are looking to other people or into the physical world for energy and validation they are dependent on the energy of others - instead of finding it within themselves. I am here to help people rediscover what they already know but have forgotten. There are many others incarnated in a human body right now just like me, who are of service helping in this way.

Time as you know and understand it, is a false construct. Meaning that linear time is for the purpose of your experience in matter *(a physical body)* along a continuous timeline. You live your life along a certain timeline that you are "plugged in to" so it appears to be one continuous experience; and you only seem to perceive what is happening along this particular timeline that your physical body can perceive. Past, present and future... brilliant, right?

Actual time is circular. Meaning, everything is happening at once. This is where people will scratch their heads and say they don't get it and this gives them a headache to think about for too long. I would grant you this time to hit the pause button, but let's keep moving along anyway, shall we?

Logically speaking you are not supposed to understand. You are currently programmed, conditioned and made to forget your true nature - which is **multidimensional**. Your *true power* has been stolen or taken from you, so to speak. You are conditioned to believe against your true inner power for reasons we won't get into here. That is the subject matter of many other books. You are conditioned from the time you are born and bombarded continuously against anything perceived beyond this reality. You are operating in a dense reality that is more like a viritual reality video game. You have also forgotten you agreed to play in this grand game. Doesn't seem fair, does it?

We have all heard or known of somebody who can see, hear, taste, smell or feel beyond the veils of ordinary reality. Think of a medium or clairvoyant who can see, hear and speak to deceased loved ones for your reference. The other senses we don't hear about as often but they absolutely do exist. These abilities are considered gifts but would be more accurately described as facets of your multidimensional being as you start your journey to rediscovering and reconnecting with your soul.

Your physical body is an amazing biofeedback machine and is capable of so much more than we have ever been told, taught or shown. When you begin the journey inward the process of reconnection and rediscovery typically takes time and practice. However, during this truly auspicious period not as much time is needed as in the past and there are many who are waking up and re-establishing inner connection at extremely rapid speeds. Your experience is unique so go easy on yourself and remember, *it's a process.*

When you begin your journey inward through the practice of meditation (and there are many ways to do this), you can re-establish your connection again and begin to express more of your true nature. Remember the most important thing is to listen to your body. Your body will be your best friend in telling you what it wants and needs through this reconnection process. Your main job *is to listen*!

Everyone is different and their ability to hold more light - which will increase as your personal frequency rate increases - will depend on various things. You may need: more sleep, less sleep, more water, less sugar, less food, more food, different kinds of food, less alcohol, less exercise, more exercise, and the list goes on.

If you find other sources telling you exactly what you should be doing please by all means learn, but use your discernment because everyone is different and our body is the best source of information for what it needs *if we will only listen to it.* You probably already know that things like processed foods are not going to help your body - that is common sense.

The more you listen the more you will learn. Learning the language of our physical bodies with reactions to how we treat it, what we feed it and learning the language of physical sensations to energy around you will then lead you to learning the language of your soul - which is light. Being able to understand light means you are able to interpret information (light is information) and translate it for the logical thinking side of your brains. The way that I am able to communicate through writing (physical communication that can be seen and read by your eyes) is a good and simple example.

Once you are capable of translating the light codes you are receiving - and you are receiving codes all the time now - you are better able to understand the true nature of your being, *a spirit having a human experience*, as more than just a concept but as your true reality... ***your multidimensional reality.***

Nobody can do the inner work for you. Only you can make the decision to choose inner work. These times are truly incredible and we are fortunate enough to be living in a human body... right now.

# RECONNECTING TO YOURSELF

## *Turning Knowledge Into Wisdom*

It has been said that the best way to predict future behavior is to look at the past. Perhaps this is true if you wanted to condemn someone to repeat the same mistakes over and over. But then what hope would any of us have at growing and improving if we are constantly *expecting* similar outcomes as dictated by our past behavior?

I suppose it would be better said that if a person wanted to change their circumstances but they haven't made any obvious changes in behavior to support the intended outcome... then yes, the above statement would prove to be true. However, this is not a good model to support you actually becoming the creator or author of your own life; nor is it a good model for you to reconnect to your higher consciousness.

What if you could both agree and disagree with past behavior as a predicting factor based on your own inner knowings as they grew with wisdom? The more you convert your aquired knowledge into wisdom the better you become at making changes that will support your desired outcome.

A person who has all the knowledge in the world may appear to be extremely intelligent to many people. They may be able to score high on tests or answer trivia about many topics. However, being intelligent in this way has abolutely no guarantee of knowledge converting into wisdom... NONE!

When we take a flat and linear approach to viewing what happens to the knowledge a person aquires, but we also assume because they have this knowledge they must automatically possess wisdom, we fail to recongnize the multidimensional aspect of the very nature of our existence. We therefore, fail recognize our true selves in it's purest form.

Without this multidimensional perspective we neglect the entire process of leveling up (ascending) in our accumulation of wisdom and light. Light is also information but that is the information which opens up as our higher consciousness after we have leveled up to wisdom from our linear and experiential knowledge. This also translates to every cell in our physical bodies.

You could call it spiritual growth to keep it simple for now. I get into the details in a much more simple way in this book so you can understand that just because someone may have accumulated knowledge, that doesn't make them intelligent in a multidimensional or spiritual way and this is also, *common sense.*

I try to bring you common sense information about what's currently taking place in a way that's easy to understand. I definitely cover some heavy content and my words are layered with messages that your higher consciousness will understand, even if you've never heard of these concepts in this particular life experience.

If I speak to you now briefly about the dangers of this new *cancel culture* we are living through, you will see just how far the pendulum has swung in the opposite direction. There is always balance in the middle, please remember.

The problem with *cancelling* someone based on

something they said (perhaps even years ago), is you run the risk of holding someone accountable for past actions when the rules of engagement were different without considering the context of when they were living, including perhaps their own ignorance at that time.

I am absolutely not talking about crimes from the past or violations from established laws or rules that were in place at the time of said actions. What I am very specifically addressing is when an onslaught against a person is led *as if it were a witch-hunt* with no room for common sense and critical thought analyzing behaviors that took place since the time of the objectionable words, action or behaviors.

More specifically, if a person did or said something objectionabale years ago and also acknowledged and apologized for it taking full responsibility and most importantly, made changes to themselves that are obvious and consistent with a more desirable behavior... why on earth would it even be consider as *'fair game'* by those regurguiating how we don't tolerate such behavior in this cancel culture we currently live in?

Perhaps you should be worried about your own statements, offensive behavior and jokes you may have made yourself in the past and ask yourself if you have learned, changed, grown into a more loving and compassionate being. Remember the story about *casting the first stone* if you are blameless.

Can we not see how truly dangerous this behavior of all mighty judge and jury has become showing a clear intent for not allowing others room for personal growth? Would we not want (or *expect* in some cases) forgiveness for ourselves if we were to make (or *have made* in the past) an ignorant mistake or err in our speech?

Nobody is perfect and to jump on any band wagon without using critical thinking shows a persons lack of ability to think for themselves or use common sense discernment. Which also reflects their own unability to show forgiveness - and that is something we could all use a little more of these days across the board: *forgiveness of yourself and forgiveness of others.*

While the cleanup is going on there will be many people who refuse to look at themselves. Instead, they are quite comfortable looking outside of their lives to gossip, criticize, blame and judge others because it's perhaps too uncomfotable to look at their own lives. However, working on yourself is always a great place to start before jumping on any band wagons and scooping up your pitch forks.

Forgiveness is going to play a very large role in

our evolutionary leap. In order to make that full connection with our higher consciousness we must first be able to truly forgive ourselves. Forgiveness is actually for you and not as much for the other person, unless they ask you for it. When you truly forgive someone on the inside you are saying that you are able to move on by releasing that experience.

Do you believe destiny plays any part? Would destiny require that you are bound to repeat past behaviors even if you learned your lesson? Is it part of destiny to be *so-called* 'cancelled' for something you did before having knowledge, wisdom or even perhaps some of the rules of the game?

If you use destiny as an excuse to repeat past behaviors then your awakening is put on delay. You have the right to delay it but also remember that lessons are repeated until they are learned.

**Becoming A Sovereign Being**

For those who haven't knowingly connected with their higher selves yet:

When things don't go your way especially if you believe in destiny you often say things happen '*to you*'. What you are actually doing is setting up the '*Great*

*Excuse'* of blaming others and the outside reality for things that happen in your life. *You may not believe in destiny at all and the same would still be true.*

What is actually happening is the energy of *lack mentality* kicks in and rears its ugly and deceptive head. Lack mentality loves excuses which are actually *just ways to blame* anyone and anything outside of yourself. This mentality allows you the excuses needed for *not taking full responsibility* for all your actions; and it blinds you to the understanding that you literally attract *(and repel)* everything to yourself in your life for your experiences.

Being a **Sovereign Being** means taking full responsibility for everything in your life.

If you say you trust and have faith in a higher power and you let someone else '*take the wheel of your life*' then you absolutely haven't learned how to **take full responsibility** for your life a sovereign being. That's like saying my dead grandmother is to thank or blame when things go right or wrong *in my life.* You may choose to believe your deceased loved ones are guiding you in spirit but they certainly *do not* make daily decisions for you, nor does any other being outside of yourself.

If I thanked or blamed my grandmother - or any other ancestor or being whom has passed out of the physical vessel - then what I'm doing is setting myself up to *hand over my personal power* for decision making and free will. As a result I will always have someone to blame *(or thank)* and I can avoid personal responsibility for my actions and decisions. These are not the actions of a sovereign being with free will.

**The Point of Free Will**

When children are young they need someone to guide them. Thanking or blaming someone for guiding you is ok when you're learning how to navigate this reality. However, at some point you're able to make decisions for yourself about your own life.

There is nothing wrong with people giving advice or assistance when you need and ask for help. Problems occur when you give your personal power away if someone imposes their will or beliefs upon you. That's typically when you first become aware of your own personal power, what it means to actually be a sovereign being and then hopefully, reclaim it.

This is where a lot of people have been getting stuck.

The conditioning has been so strong that people have a hard time *challenging beliefs* that were handed to them as a child. Just because someone told you it was true, must it be so? That never, EVER *made anything true* - just because someone told you so... because someone told them it was true... That does seem very much like a hidden aspect of the *lack mentality* we were just talking about and it has been perpetuated in a very long cycle passed down through the generations.

There is a **simple solution** for people who are stuck. *It may be simple but not necessarily easy.*

**It is your birthright** to *use your given rights* to:

*Think freely* by suspending core beliefs imposed upon you from childhood and by society in general.

*Due your due diligence* by searching out information that supports both sides of any belief system.

*Learn from personal experience* and by what you have now researched (not just what you heard and were told by anyone).

Suspend *disbeliefs of everything* you previously thought wasn't *or couldn't* be true.

And finally, *make adjustments* to what feels right in your heart center for establishing new beliefs that better fit you as an adult (*yes, it's your feelings that will guide you to truth*).

Always ask yourself, ***"Does this resonate with me?"*** Listen with your heart and you will know if something *feels right* or not - if it **resonates** with you or not.

You can start making decisions for yourself based on beliefs from your own personal experiences (not someone else's) and your very own inner knowing. You really do have a personal guidance system inside but it's up to you to activate and use it. The default switch is set to autopilot and only you can shift to manual.

** Remember, ***it's not what you know, but what you use of what you know*** that ultimately matters. Full disclosure: I found that saying in a fortune cookie and I carry it around with me to this day reminding me to use my gifts as often as possible.

Eventually little humans become full-grown humans but their bodies don't always reflect their maturity level. Spiritual maturity comes from experiences that allow for inner growth.

**Spoiler Alert:** You can choose inner growth at any time during your human incarnation.

**Feeling Blocked From Your True *Inner Connection*.**

When someone says they are blocked from their true inner connection or they can't seem to connect to their higher selves this so simple to fix. First let's understand that these blocks are in place by your own creation. Second these blocks from your inner self are rooted deep in confusion.

Where there is doubt there is a default mechanism that kicks in from this confusion. This is important. *It's a self-generated program created from the conditioning received as a child.* These **default blocks** actually take over our decision making processes tricking us into thinking a true inner connection isn't real or that we are somehow broken. They are automatically activated when there *appears to be* a threat to your core belief systems.

In most cases the habits resulting from the beliefs imprinted upon us as little children block our perceived ability to search for inner truth. A lot of the humans on this planet are taught to trust someone or something outside of ourselves. But how can we ever make that inner connection 'work' again if we're always looking outside of ourselves for validation and truth?

This is how a lot of us got stuck without our true self identities and knowingness of how to get out. Our inner connection was switched off. The good news is that we have the personal and collective power to reprogram ourselves and reestablish our inner guidance systems. Let's talk about the game.

## Hide and Seek Is A Fun Childhood Game

If you know and understand joy when you bring your inner child out to play then why not look at life as a big game of hide and seek! The goal is to find yourself - *your true higher self* - and nobody can do it for you but you can have friends give you hints where to look.

You have been told your heart is the secret hiding place many times but never quite understood how to get there because you have these old blocks.

You started the game but you have given up because the game was rigged and you felt alone in your search for far to long. You knew as a child how to connect but your protective mechanisms took over and you have long since forgotten.

If you give up too soon you stop learning the truly important lessons.

Games are fun and learning can be fun too when you remember life is really just a game. Mind you, a very, VERY long and tiring game who has seen many opponents cheat and play dirty *(but that's another story).*

When you choose to engage with the game again, **you can learn from experience and gain knowledge.**

Try to see knowledge as points in the game. You get the points when you learn lessons. In this game your points need to be converted so you can level up. You must choose to level up willingly. Nobody can do this for you - that's the big secret and the key to success in this game.

### How The Spiritual Maturity Process Works While In Your Human Incarnation

You *choose to engage* in learning (actively playing the game of life).

You *gain knowledge* (points) because lessons are learned and personal experienced is achieved.

You have *suspended all core beliefs* that were given to you as a child or by someone else.

You are now *choosing your own beliefs,* congratulations!

You *convert your knowledge (points) into wisdom* (leveling up) by accepting full responsibility for everything in your life and *move forward with this under-*

*standing.*

You will then be able to *find and connect with your higher self(s).* Yes, there is more than one but let's just start with reconnecting in your heart center with the first one who is closest in vibration to you.

This process doesn't mean your life is perfect and lessons won't continue. As long as you are in a human body you can continue your spiritual growth.

The knowledge you gain along your journey is written within the unique blueprint of your heart (literally) and will mature into wisdom when you decide to use it. Eventually little humans become full-grown but their bodies don't necessarily reflect their spiritual maturity level. So let's talk about how we get signs for spiritual development through triggering events.

◆ ◆ ◆

### Triggers Are Important Signs

Spiritual maturity starts to develop *when you are capable* of suspending core beliefs that were forced upon you as a child. You then begin to engage in *true self-learning.* Knowledge can also come from navigating events that trigger you with a sincere desire to change old habits which no longer serve you. However, first you must recognize and desire to really get into your triggers; not avoid them or use them as excuses as to why you are avoiding certain feelings or situations.

It's becoming common among the younger generations to use the word 'trigger' as an avoidance mechanism. This is alarming because instead of really getting into why you are triggered in the first place and *fully dealing* with those emotions and feelings *(yes, it can be scary)* nothing will be learned until they are properly addressed and healed inside.

Just knowing your triggers doesn't translate to knowledge in spiritual terms, nor will it convert into wisdom until the lessons are achieved. **Remember: *lessons are repeated until they are learned*.** Why continue this cycle knowingly? There is a saying, "*there is nothing to fear except fear itself*" and this would apply quite well in this example.

I've heard a lot of people say things like "*that triggered me...*" or "*I can't see (or watch) that because it will trigger my anxiety...*". People seem well aware of their triggers but they stop short of doing the inner work to heal the cause. Those peopel are (most times) very well aware of which group of feelings they're avoiding. They are actively choosing not to engage in the healing process.

## Why Would Anyone Avoid Healing?

If something triggers you then ***there's something worth checking out.*** It might feel like a side road but it's definitely a flashing light saying something wants and needs to be healed and released. It's like finding a bonus item in the middle of a game. It's *a loud and clear signal* for you to **gain something** and it's literally shouting at you to look at it and pick it up - really get into it and learn something about yourself.

Learning the value of overcoming adversity and becoming stronger *is priceless in wisdom* but there's still a price to pay. Not all beings here right now have been willing to pay the heavy price that comes with a large amount of challenges and adversity. A lot are trying but having an easy life seems much more appealing on the surface. However, there's not as much opportunity for growth and to convert knowledge into wisdom from an 'easier' life.

Try to see your triggers as bright and shiny objects offering you the promise of some major points that can be converted into wisdom, *literally being handed to you if only you would pick it up and look at it*!

There could be much value to something you pick up along the way, *if only you are willing* to take a closer look.

It could be **something you need to forgive** within yourself.
It could be **something you haven't addressed** yet.
It could be **fear that's ready to be released**.
It could be **pain that needs to be healed**.
I could be **sadness that needs to be comforted.**
It could be **an old memory that needs to be set free.**
It could be a **lesson you have been avoiding**.
It could be **a challenge you haven't accepted** yet.
*And so on...*

Or it could be ***a signal for the next chapter****...*

It could also be your life's mission, soul contract or part of your original blueprint to gain a certain 'knowledge base' and then the triggers come when it's time for the *next-level maturity* to occur - because you have reached a certain point of transcending previous levels of information (or perhaps wisdom) and now you are ready for the next step. *** *Cue the triggers for the most stubborn sleepy ones who keep hitting the snooze button on their spiritual evolution.*

But rest assured that a release *always occurs* both

when the time and the person are right. Is that considered *DESTINY?*

If you are a person who says you believe in destiny and *everything* that happens in your life *must be* someone (or something) else's will, are you not just avoiding doing the work here on this free will planet? The 'work' also involves getting to know your true self and remembering where you came from.

Yes, actually remembering and reconnecting with your higher self and integrating that higher power *within you*. It's not on the outside and no other person living in a human body can or should *'do it for you'*. Taking responsibility for your life is a *sovereign being, free will* choice that YOU have to make.

You can avoid it or you can start looking within your own heart. Sitting on a fence that no longer exists is silly.

## CONTROLLERS BEWARE! YOU ARE PUT ON NOTICE - WE SEE YOU!

Micromanaging people is simply another version of controlling people and trying to impose your will. Often people who do this actually feel no control in their own lives. They use this technique without realizing awakened people can see it a mile away and very often reject it. We work with people like this only when we must - and we infuse as much love energy as we can.

The person doing the controlling will often feel like the other person is being difficult when in fact, they are simply *exercising* their ***sovereign right not be controlled***. Blaming others by using the Great Excuse is a sign that you haven't matured in spirit yet and both micromanaging and blaming are quite obvious to those who are already awakened.

Perhaps you have noticed some people just seem to fall out of your life. I assure you that when your energy levels 'uplift' in rate of vibration you will no longer want to be around people, situations and things that steal your energy (knowingly or unknowingly). Everyone must figure out how to make their own reconnection to Source within their own heart centers.

Your heart is not just an organ that keeps your physical body alive by pumping blood through your system. It's a very real energetic center that can be viewed as your own personal portal to higher dimensions. This is where you make your reconnection. It does translate into your physical vessel which you can see with your spiritual eyes. If your eyes are not yet opened then perhaps it's time!

**Reconnecting is your goal right now.**

For those who have or are in the process of connecting with their higher selves: When you look at your free will choices to co-create your life... *are you using your gifts to be of service*?

There comes a point in the process of ascending where you know what you know and that's enough because life is hard in this reality. You've had enough. You just want to go home. You are tired of dealing with people who drain your energy. And then it happens again and again, over and over.

Remember this and I will say it one more time: **Lessons are repeated until they are learned**. Just because you reconnected with your higher self doesn't mean your life will be perfect. It doesn't mean you won't feel hurt, pain and suffering. You are human and you are supposed to feel and feel *FULLY!*

The questions then becomes, "*how do you react or respond to what you feel?*" Do you react with knee-jerk reactions when you get triggered? If so, most likely there is still something inside that needs healing and release. Perhaps you haven't released everything from that hurt, pain or traumatic memory you've worked on for years and years and let go of many times (*and still get triggered*). There are many layers to the onion just as there are many layers to you with your hurts and pains. Don't avoid your triggers.

Healing triggers leads to healing old wounds. Healing in this way will lead to your destiny points. It's the time factor that's more fluid since it doesn't (really) exist - not the way you've been taught.

Destiny points are very real indeed. Free will allows you to choose which path your human ego will take that eventually leads to true destiny points. Fluidity in destiny points allows for circular time (true time/no-time) to adjust to linear time (false time) on this planet but all paths will eventually lead you back home. **It's up to you as to how long you play the game** of life. Finding yourself in this game **is still your objective.**

Will you continue to hit your head with a hammer over and over if it causes pain? It's your choice but the longer you do that the longer your healing will take. Your destiny point of healing is already a true destiny point. *You just have to figure out when it's right for you to achieve this.*

# DREAMS

## *The Key To Your Inner Child*

When you follow your dreams do you feel you must sacrifice other areas of your life in order to do so? Do you ever feel like you're just going through the motions wondering what's the point to everything? Have you discovered this reality to be the actual dream reality yet? Do you remember your nightly travels?

Seems like some very different topics but *what if they're actually related?*

It's horrible that people are so drained these days after coming home from their jobs. They often just want to relax and unwind. And who can blame anyone for wanting to do that? I love to take time for myself and have a healthy dose of R&R. I actually consider this a requirement for a healthy balance. But it's very easy to get stuck in either *work* or *relax-*

*ation* mode.

**We all go through it!**

Sometimes it's seasonal. Sometimes it seems to cycle with the moon. Sometimes it's just about what's going on in our daily lives or around the world. I go through periods of wanting nothing more than to just rest - when the weight of the world feels too heavy to go on. I love binge watching Netflix. I love sleeping in and not having to wake up to a loud and obnoxious alarm... who doesn't?

We need those rest periods but those periods aren't meant to be all the time, night after night in front of the TV, computer or smartphone. Finding extra time to do the things I wanted to set in motion was a huge challenge the first time I ever tried back in my twenties with four young children. I had many late nights writing, editing and teaching myself HTML code when the Internet was just getting started.

I was hungry to learn and was a sponge back then. Like Elon Musk recently said on twitter, *life was much simpler back when (he) was a sponge.*

I had a new plan.

Well, not really a plan but I had inspiration from

my oldest son who unfortunately and most surprisingly, crossed over to the other side in March of 2018. This time I was going *'all-in'* with a lifelong passion... Art and energy healing - combined! This was finally my life's work all coming together.

*Why didn't I see this before?* Because everything unfolds exactly when it's supposed to. My plan was one thing but there was a much larger plan under it all - it's called Divine Timing.

My son has been making sure I'm well aware that he's still very much alive. I visit him in my nightly travels. Not as often as I wish but nevertheless he is in a place *I know is very real.* It even feels *MORE REAL* than this reality. If you can understand that then you probably have experienced this place as well.

I write in other places about dream travels and visiting non-ordinary reality. For now, ordinary reality is being defined as basically *this physical 3rd dimensional* world. Everything else is considered non-ordinary reality for simplicity. In my other writings I describe how travel outside your physical body is a very real thing. Your mind is most definitely not playing tricks on you.

At night when your body fall asleep you can go out and about traveling to other realities where other parts of yourself are inhabiting - located *all over* this multiverse. Travel does have its limits but you can and do, pop into your other aspects' consciousness. Sometimes you can remember your dreams, sometimes you can't. Some people claim they can't or don't dream.

**This is false. Everyone dreams. Not everyone remembers.**

If you are dependent on any substances or medications you may have a more difficult time with recalling your dream memories. There are several other reasons why people have memory blocks but some medications can be a problem while others can reportedly induce very intense or strange dreams. If you are serious about recalling your nightly travels then there's plenty of actions you can take to make this discipline a fun journey of self discovery.

When my son started making appearances in my dreams *after he crossed over,* it seemed no different than ordinary reality. I have always dreamed with him and my other children so it all seemed quite normal but ***very*** welcomed. When I first realized (over 'there' in non-ordinary reality) that he had died (over 'here' in ordinary reality) it was very strange because I knew 'over there' that *this 'life' here, was only a dream! I KNEW IT with every part of me!*

**This is not the first time *I've been in non-ordinary reality and known 'this life' to be a dream*.**

However, this was the first time 'over there' dreaming with my son that I truly and fully embraced this realization. In that particular 'experience' I was with all my children, including my oldest. *Why was nobody talking about the elephant in the room,* I thought. I said to him, *"But James, you died over there!"* as if I was revealing some big secret. He just looked at me with a smile on his face and said, *"Yes, yes I did."*

I thought he didn't understand what I was saying, so naturally I repeated it with more emphasis. He answered me again and this time I felt my arms, I felt my body and I knew it to be a very, VERY real place; and I knew our lives (here) were more like a game. A game that seemed very real and a game that he was *taken out of* and was no longer to play the role as an incarnated human.

Over there he was simply out of *'the game'* we call human life on Earth. You can call it a school but if you try to think of life more as a game, I promise it's better.

Who *really* has fun in school? Games are fun. Life is supposed to be fun. We have lost something along the way and we need to remember how to have fun again.

If we all just live life fearing death then it's not fully possible to have fun, now is it? A lot of people fear their death and I ask you this, *WHY?*

**Death Is A Doorway**

Death is the door for you to leave this body and return to who you truly are - the much bigger part of you that decided to come down here and play this Earth game. If you choose to pay money to go into a game (like a session of paintball, or time on the bouncy bounce blow up thing, or a VR game) and the person in charge sets the timer... you don't know exactly when times up because you are fully immersed in your game or session.

*You still chose to go into the game with a full knowing that the purpose was to fully experience it, have fun and enjoy it!*

**When life is a game things change. It's all perspective.**

We start to reconnect with our inner child again. That child has been told by the world it needs to stay locked up in some dingy closet to stay safe... *'be-*

*cause the world is a cruel and dangerous place'.*

This world is also a wondrous place. It was meant for us to explore, to have fun and to learn lessons. We are supposed to do things and fall forward so we can learn while gaining experiences. Not to stay locked up in our closets hiding from everyone and everything that *could possibly* hurt us.

*Do we get hurt?* **Darn right we do!** *Does that mean we don't try things another way?* **Heck no!** *Why give up?*

If giving up means I have to sleep in all the time and binge watch TV every night, then I may as well just leave now. There's no point to wasting my life when I can actually be living it, making mistakes, getting back up and allowing myself to get hurt again. *Why allow myself to get hurt again?* Certainly not because I enjoy it but because *that's how we learn and grow.*

If you have something you want to do, try, experience, try again another way... why not just do it? Every single person came here with unique gifts to share. Every. Single. Person. *What are you doing with you gifts? How are you pursuing your dreams - something you are passionate about?* Even if you have to initially make some sleep adjustments (i.e. going to bed later or waking up earlier to have 'more time') it's definitely worth it and you can do it! Think about what your purpose is - what you are passionate about - and you will find all you need to get on *(or back on)* your path.

◆ ◆ ◆

**Learning Gives You Knowledge**

I'll remind you about that fortune cookie message I received saying, *"It's not what you know but what you use of what you know that matters"*. One of the reasons I still carry that with me is because it also reminds me to stay hungry for knowledge. The more you use your knowledge the more experience you get. The more experience you get the more your knowledge ages into wisdom as you mature and consciously choose to level up.

**Making life a game requires an inner hunger to do better.**

No matter how bad life seems, (believe me I'm speaking from experience) no matter how *BAD* it gets... you can always find joy in little gestures and actions that require no money and no status. This requires the heart of your inner child. Set them free from that dingy inner-closet and find out for yourself!

If you're feeling like you got the crap beat out of you recently, perhaps its time to make a move off that couch and take a break from the boob tube. I promise your shows can be watched at a later time - *or not at all if you're really going for it. You have something to do before your time is up! We all do...* so stop allowing the literal 'programs' to control you and your life.

Sometimes you just need a break from the matrix constructs that say you *SHOULD do this,* or you *SHOULD do that.* Stop *"should-ing"* all over yourself and free your mind. You are a sovereign being and you can claim that freedom again by taking actions *by choice* instead of responding with reactions and conditioning ('should-ing').

If you decide to start the discipline of recalling your nightly travels which can help you immensely in pursuing your dreams, get yourself a journal or recording device if you don't want to write. Say out loud that you *WILL remember your dreams* multiple times before bed and as you're drifting off to sleep. Set your intention.

Most importantly, upon awakening be still for a few moments and ask yourself these questions multiple times before your ego/personality mind takes over - pausing after each question:

*1) Where was I just at?*

*2) What was I just doing?*

*3) What was I just feeling?*

This works even if you don't initially remember. Don't let your monkey mind tell you *"ahh you never remember..."* just say those 3 questions again and let it go. When you make a decision to do this as a discipline you will see results.

When a memory pops up it will typically be like a screenshot. *You got it now!* Then you ask yourself, *"Where was I coming from or where was I just at prior to (insert the screenshot memory)*?" and let the memories expand.

I personally use this technique when I wake with little to no memory and they **always come back** before I finish in the bathroom. I actually spend between 15-30 minutes most mornings writing down my dreams. And it helps me navigate my time here. I get a lot of information from non-ordinary reality and it really does help me integrate my higher self and pursue my dreams in this reality.

**Anyone can do this!**

I'm gifting you my best technique for dream recall when you don't automatically have it upon awakening. Use it well. Treat it with respect. I take dream work very seriously and have been actively practicing since 1992.

People ask me all the time about dream work. This simple technique really works and can help you with recalling your memories too, when you're ready to dive into the practice. I hope it helps anyone who wants to remember their dreams and start active participation in non-ordinary reality.

# THE STORM IS COMING

◆◆◆

It has been said there is a calm before the storm. If you have been paying attention then you know it's coming... and not a few years or even a few months from now but it's already underway. With this storm there is a cleansing that is so desperately needed in so many areas and on so many levels. It's an ongoing purification.

It is and will be, welcomed by many even if it requires some perceived hardships - when it brings **Truth** then it will be welcomed.

It has been a long time coming. Generally speaking, healing and forgiveness can not take place until truth is revealed. The truth needs to come out so we, as a species, can finally learn ***the truth about our origins***. Once we learn the truth then (and only then) can we hold those accountable for their horrendous crimes against humanity, which - *believe it or not* - does include having a compassionate, loving and forgiving heart.

Forgiveness is actually meant for you not the being you are forgiving. First, **you must learn how to forgive yourself** *before* you can forgive others.

**Have you mastered that yet?**

There will be a lot of forgiveness needed once people realize how fooled, conditioned, hypnotized and used they truly have been. There will also be quite a bit of anger to go around.

And then we have blame. There will be no shortage of that. However, let's not forget ***we are*** **ALL responsible** *for our thoughts, actions and behaviors.*

When people stop to evaluate how incredibly inhumane they have treated their fellow citizens because of these lies *and because they have chosen not to see the truth*, they may want to isolate and blame instead of taking full responsibility for their actions.

If you committed crimes against humanity then you need to make it right and atone for your crimes. If you unknowingly contributed to said crimes there will be ways to re-balance your karma and that will all be explained to you when the time is right. If you participated in actions that would discredit others trying to bring forth the truth, then you know how to start the self-forgiveness process and start balancing your actions.

Other actions by individuals that include public shaming, discrediting, taunting, emotional abuse, etc. can all be addressed by first stopping that behavior and then forgiving yourself. You will move on to balancing all the karma you created for yourself after you recognize what you have done, taken responsibility for it and begin the repair process within yourself first, then others.

But above all else we must learn to listen with our hearts, treat others the way we want to be treated (and that includes how we actively treat ourselves) and then we must practice forgiveness when we are ***integrating the Truth*** about all that is (coming...) and currently being revealed; it is *then* when *we actually live awakened* in the Golden Age together trusting once more and addressing the issues of this beautiful planet which need immediate attention.

We serve this planet and we serve each other.

# MOVING FORWARD

## *In Times Unknown*

Moving forward can feel like the most challenging thing to do when you're in the middle of being stuck to your feelings. Those feelings could be considered attachments, but we'll take a peek at attachments later. For now just ask yourself, *"do my feelings control me or do I actively use them as a tool?"*

What do I mean when I say, "*use them as a tool*"? Let's start by asking if you consider your feelings to be annoying, startling, scary, hard to handle, too much or even, overwhelming? Or do you have a handle on reading your feelings as they come in, like a personal guidance system?

If you don't see beyond the physical 3D material world yet, try to imagine the energy as constantly moving, like a body of water. Now put yourself in this body of water and you have life in your body here on Earth. If you don't know how to swim you will probably swallow some water and cough a bit when a wave passes, most likely.

***Learning how to swim is part of the waking up process.***

Floating is a skill you develop along the way after you can see and accept the water you are in. Once you can keep your head above the water you can learn how to float with the waves. You use less energy when you are able to float and it actually becomes more enjoyable as you learn how to relax into it.

While floating, you can begin to sense when larger waves are coming from the currents and pulls of the water. The really large ones are obvious and most people - *even those still sleeping* - can feel when something really big is approaching.

As you realize you are part of the eternal body of ocean/energy/life, you start to reach out to test your skills. You may let your ears dip into the water and you notice you can hear better. You may drop your head in entirely and even dare to open your eyes! Perhaps you have a pair of goggles so you have no fear of burning your eyes.

Along the way, you may have something float across your path like a life vest or something to hang on to. You also may have been clinging to this 'life vest' the entire time because you were always told you could drown in deep water. You were also told to fear what you can't see.

You have never put your head in the water because this flotation device has stopped you and given you a false sense of being safe. Therefore, you haven't developed any extra senses that you can call upon at will.

**Your muscles have become weak because of your clinging.**

You have also become lazy from your lack of strengthening your muscles by swimming every day. You failed to learn how to bob up and down because you feared going down under to far. You fear going down under because you listened to the programming and other people that said it wasn't safe, *instead of listening to your own heart and internal guidance.*

You feel scared and alone. Like nobody understands how tired you have become.

All you want is for that rescue boat to come and get you. Other times when you float really high over a very enjoyable wave, you feel elated and can't help but wonder what else could be waiting for you in this great big body of water.

**How did you even get here? *Why* are you here?**

You have questions and you want answers. Not much else really matters except the truth. Along the way you have met many other beings in the water. Some look like you and others look very different. Some can swim better than others and some even can hold their breath for a very, very long time.

You have made many friends along the way but ultimately you always wind up by yourself - because nobody can swim *for you.* Even after you make some promises that you will travel to the end of the journey with others, sometimes you wake up after sleeping a bit and they are gone. Often times they just drift away when a wave passes through.

You have become accustomed to all of it and you start to feel like the journey will never end.

*It will End. It always does so something new and different can be explored.*

A really large wave passes by and you see something from the very top. You're not sure what it is but you remember a homeland and it starts to jolt your memories.

You make a decision to master the skills needed to keep swimming. You no longer want to wait for a rescue. You decide it's up to you to get in line with the waves so you can begin to actually ride them to your destination.

**You want to learn how to surf!**

You want to feel everything there is to feel. You want to hear all the sounds in the water. You want to see the truth of everything there is to see beyond the veil of where the water meets the air. You know there is more because you not only trust, but you have memories of when you've had a taste of it before and you long for it again.

The process of waking up occurs with ALL. Everyone will wake up one way or another. It's easier to do it (here) when you are aware of *'deciding to'* do it. There may come a time soon when a huge wave beyond all waves pulses us into a new vibration and cannot be denied by any still blind and deaf in the heart... but before that event takes place there is much work to be done.

People are NOW currently wide awake, aware and living in multidimensional reality while in their bodies. And more are making the connection with their Source and higher consciousness everyday! No longer can people lie, for it can be seen and felt by those awakened already. The world is changing rapidly.

When you feel overwhelmed by your feelings just remember this: you are learning how to use them as your personal guidance system. No longer is it viable to deny feelings or let them control you. Let go, move forward bravely and trust you are Divinely guided.

The tools are VERY SIMPLE: As soon as you start to feel overwhelmed...

1) Breath deeply and deliberately.

2) Imagine LIGHT and breath that into the top of your head. Bring it down through your body - especially through your heart and out your feet into Earth.

3) Bring light (by breathing) to the source of your discomfort.

4) Exhale negative energy.

YOU GOT THIS! We're all in this together.

# LET YOUR GIFTS BE SHARED AND MULTIPLIED

◆ ◆ ◆

The times you are living through right now are truly unprecedented. There is no user manual for what we are all either experiencing or about to experience. If you can suspend all disbelief for just a few moments you still might have a hard time understanding what's taking place across this planet.

When you were a child you used your imagination for just about everything. That ability was almost destroyed in a lot of people through all the conditioning on your planet. People frequently say they "*can't imagine*" or they "*have a hard time*" imagining even the smallest things. Other people say they "*can't see*" something with their eyes closed.

If you are closing your eyes and seeing darkness, that's fine. But what else do you see? Some people report specks of light, flashes of light, orbs and other types of light... but I'm not talking about clairvoyance at the moment.

**I am referring to your inner sight.**

The screen inside your mind that allows you to perceive what your imaginations hold the key to - that realm of sight on the inside that your consciousness is connected to... If you are expecting to see everything with your physical eyes then that is all you will see.

But *when you suspend your disbeliefs you are able to perceive the inner sight we all have access to,* ***limitless sight using your consciousness and energy bodies - not just your physical eyes.***

Communications from the 'spirit world' (to keep terms simple) is often given to you through images and impressions. These impressions are actually packets of information distributed to you in a way that you can understand and comprehend.

At least, that is the challenge of your guides, angels, higher selves or whatever label you wish to use for a being that is not corporeal (physical). They need to communicate from a dimension or realm that is not as dense as this physical world.

Understand that dimensions are separated by frequency bands, similar to your radio and television stations in the third dimension. You can tune in to each frequency by changing the station; same as you can tune in to various dimensions by changing your frequency. The more you practice the more efficient you will get with your perceptions.

Everyone is capable of tuning in to various frequencies.

Your consciousness can and does transcend multiple layers of frequencies all the time. You are a multidimensional being and your physical body was designed to do this. Try to think of it as a biofeedback system that gives you signals in response to stimuli which can come from any and all of your senses.

### Explaining Your Sixth Sense

You have five physical senses and when you realize how to use these senses properly all of your senses become heightened exponentially and then they become the package that is referred to as your sixth sense.

Think of your sixth sense as a graduation for your five senses. They become members of your team - active crew members on your ship who all work together and you are the captain of your human vessel ship, which sails the seas on the endless ocean of the universe (or multiverse).

Once you realize you are a spiritual being having a human experience you can then move to accept that you are a multidimensional being - and your body was designed for your greatest experience. If you are not your body but simply 'wearing it' while on this planet, why would you be designed to only have five physical senses that only worked with the body in the physical realm?

**You are so much more than you have been conditioned to believe.**

Your senses were designed for you to openly communicate with your higher aspects, the spirit world, other dimensions - and everything on your stream of consciousness - directly to the Creator Source of all that is. You most likely can "sense" what you are reading or hearing is true - and you probably resonate or recognize the frequency with which I speak - and know this already in the energetic centers that are located in your heart.

So you can start to recognize your innate abilities

and have a better understanding of what's coming up for you over the next period of your life, here is a basic list of the *clairs* for you:

**Clairvoyance** - *clear seeing.* This does not necessarily mean you only see energy and auras. Most people don't realize that clairvoyants get mental pictures and flashes of mental images that provide insight. Often times someone with these natural abilities may not realize their gifts are already 'online'. These visions and images are both in your ***outer and your inner world***.

**Clairaudience** - *clear hearing.* The ability to hear voices, sounds and cues from other dimensions can come from both your ***outer hearing and your inner hearing.*** This is another example of how someone may not understand their gifts are 'active' and they think their inner *'chatter'* is just noise that won't stop. They may not be able to sleep at night or find traditional meditation challenging because their inner noise seems to be impossible to shut down. (*When in fact, their gifts are becoming more active.*) These people would benefit greatly from learning how to best develop and use it so they can set proper boundaries and regain their inner peace.

**Clairtangency** - *clear feeling (tactile).* Being able to touch an object and perceive information from the energy in that object. Think of psychometry.

**Clairsalience** - *clear smelling.* This gift is when you receive information through your sense of smell. The smell is not actually something others around you can perceive. It comes from other dimensions and your heightened sense of smell allows you to receive information through this sense.

**Clairgustance** - *clear tasting.* This gift gives you insight through a sudden taste in your mouth which triggers information to be downloaded to your consciousness.

When you start the awakening process, you become aware that you have a tendency towards one or maybe two of these clairs that are more dominant. Once your start to see how these all work together, *you can develop stronger clairs that encompass a more total body awareness such as:*

**Clairempathy** - *the ability to feel the emotions of others.* Healers often have this gift most of their lives and most likely identify with this gift quite naturally. It may be the first clair they recognize within themselves. Empaths often suffer much before recognizing they are feeling others pain, etc. They can then learn how to discern, block, transmute and tune in to others emotions during their journey with this gift active.

**Clairsentience** - *the ability to clearly feel and ex-*

*perience energy and other signals through your body.* Those with this active gift will be able to confirm a truth they are speaking by experiencing chills in a certain area of their body. They can also learn to discern truth from other people through physical sensations in their body. They are able to identify the energetic signatures of spiritual beings by knowing the feelings in their bodies. Sensations are varied and can be hot, cold, warm, wet, tingles, chills, etc. Much information can be said about this gift but know that *it's always working*, you just need to learn how to *listen to your body* and *become more aware of what it's saying to you.*

**Claircognizance** - *the ability to clearly know things* in an instant - like a sudden insight out of nowhere. This is an innate ability that is every persons' birthright. Once you start the awakening process and recognize you have these gifts, you practice and get better by trusting your senses.

When you unlock and open up several of these gifts you eventually recognize that you just start knowing things. There is no explanation for how you know the things you do but you are just given information when you need it the most and voila, it is there for you.

The gift of claircognizance comes with the ability to trust your higher consciousness, your higher selves, your soul, and the Creator Source of all that is.

Now is the time for everyone to expand their consciousness, trust their senses, get deep in your inner world and allow your birthrights to blossom on your very own Tree of Life.

The time for expansion *is now*

The time to trust yourselves *is now*

The time to share your gifts *is now*

The time to dust off your dreams and offer what you have *is now*

Trust that **you are enough** and that your piece to the puzzle is equally valuable. You are here and you all have a part to play.

# WHAT IS REAL?

*Let's take a dive into non-ordinary reality! A very deep dive.*

Ordinary reality is being defined here as the constructs (we, as a collective) agree is the physical world. Non-ordinary reality is being defined here, as everything else.

People have been taking their consciousness to places where our physical bodies can't go for as long as you can imagine.

If you don't understand this or actually, if it triggers you to hear that people can leave their bodies, travel to very real places and remember their journeys (with or without the help of any particular substances), then I'm advising you to stop reading right now and skip to the next chapter. Why get yourself triggered or upset with insights that could possibly challenge your entire belief structures if you're not willing to suspend disbeliefs? If you choose to continue reading whether or not you believe the content you are requested to be respectful while listening to your heart and while processing the following information in this section. It comes from a higher consciousness and is formatted in a slightly different way.

*If people travel and they don't take their bodies does this mean they didn't really go anywhere but rather, the brain is playing a trick?* Absolutely not.

*Is Astral travel what you're taking about?* That is one way.

*Can everyone everyone astral project?* Some people have this happen spontaneously while others can learn by practicing. But this is not the subject of importance today. Astral projection is not what you are here to do at this time.

*Can you travel when you are meditating?* Absolutely. This is the way shamans, healers and many others traverse on their journeys.

*Do you need some sort of psychedelic drug or a substance to alter your brain so you can travel?* I will say this: you do not need anything to travel. Just the act of sleeping at night takes you out of your body and you travel to non-ordinary realities. Some have better recall of their nightly travels for various reasons. When a being begins to wake up and consciously decides to start the discipline needed to recall accurate memories from their travels, they may also choose to experiment with different substances in order to shift their perspective and push their consciousness to an altered reality while they are awake and aware. It is simply easier for them to remember the experience. Not everyone does this. Dream work takes a long time to develop and master and typically needs a additional dedication to writing - these pair well together. Although recording technology can also be used. The major benefit to dream travel is that you actually project into what you're calling non-ordinary reality and experience 'you' in your other very real bodies and realities.

*So it's true, you do travel in your dream state?* You know this is absolutely true.

*Ha-ha. I was asking for my readers. This is the first time we've formatted like this - as a question and answer type of way. Normally, you will just stream through me while I write. I'm wondering why this is different now. Can you shed any light?* I am not the only being who streams through you while you write. You had a dream you awoke from this morning and you had questions. You wrote all the details down and you had an excellent recall from your travels. There is important information about your journey and you are stepping out of your inhibitions about sharing your experiences. This format works for the messages we want to convey.

*OK, wow, thank you. How do you want me to share this?* Write out the full dream and ask your most important questions.

*Here goes... as written in my dream journal and only edited for clarity.*

~ I was at some facility. It was a resting place for people that have probably just crossed over and there was a vast variety of issues. There were a lot of evaluations taking place and I didn't like being observed. It felt, off.

I remember being there a little while, like I had the memory of being there for at least a few weeks maybe longer. I was saying something about not arranging things anymore for everyone (like in an OCD kind of way). Apparently I was arranging things to be used as grids.

I was telling one of the observers that I wasn't going to do that anymore because this was not my home. Although I was starting to feel more comfortable in my room and was still making grids there.

There was a group observation of a young girl

and they were inspecting her private parts under a sheet. I felt uncomfortable because I thought they were making porn, until they showed everyone she had male parts. Then I could see she was actually supposed to be in a girl body, but was not. I left and went to her private room where she was now in a boys body and her mother was there. Her mother told me, *"She knew she was supposed to be a girl. From the time she could talk she told us, she was a girl"*

The mother showed me a memory of how they said it. It was basically some of their first verbal sentences, *"I'm girl"*! The mother was showing me how this was done on purpose. I immediately understood who the group was that were doing these things at that facility. And they have been very, very naughty!

I went back to my room and this was one of the reasons why I was so upset and knew I didn't belong there. A female observer was in my room trying to get me to talk about it and I started to explain energy layers. I was describing it as basic as I could. I asked her and others that were listening, to imagine a square room.

I started describing how energy moves in layered waves. One right on top of the other. I also told them they weren't necessarily the same distance apart from each other. As I was about to make some serious points, my sister decided it was time to go.

Right now!

She was apparently also in this place or a being who looked like her. When I started to get ready I had also been having a conversation about orbs with the female observer, she had a few experiences as well. I was prevented from showing my videos of orbs and was told I had to leave right at that moment.

I heard the male and female observers going back and forth about something. I heard the male become demeaning to the female. I heard nothing back from the female. I decided this was not OK and spoke up.

He sort of mocked me at first until I told him that I didn't care how old his was, I was married (and divorced) twice and I knew **this was wrong** - they way he was talking to the female. I woke up shortly after.
~

*My questions are direct. Was I at a place where people go when they die, some sort of facility?* Yes. But the one you visited was being dismantled.

*Why was it being dismantled?* Because it was for the sole purpose of falsely conditioning beings between incarnations and putting them into the wrong bodies. They were debriefing and reconditioning beings with false karma and false gender identification.

*What do you mean by that? Can you explain a little more please?* Yes. In between your lifetimes you are debriefed and prepared for your next. You are shown what karma needs to be resolved and a blueprint or plan is presented. Included in that plan is a gender choice that would best benefit you to resolve said karma. These plans are supposed to be handled over much longer rest and integration periods and done in conjunction with a much higher aspect of yourself in the least traumatic way possible.

This particular facility was a very dark place with the appearance of the helping type of afterlife facilities. Many beings were tricked into going there upon death falling victim to their agenda. They pushed you through as fast as possible, showed you false information thereby tricking you into thinking you have karma which was in fact, not yours. And finally, they were putting people into the wrong bodies after all the contracts were signed and they were on their way to be incarnated. This had to stop. This is why it is being dismantled. It was all done with black magic. There is a HUGE control force on your planet disguised as a very large church which is also being dismantled. I can not give any more information about this except to say it is all part of disclosure and the world will watch in both joy and disbelief at what is being revealed.

*I understand the disbelief, but why joy?* Because those who have been working towards disclosing truth and ushering in the Golden Age will understand and know it is really happening and feel a huge joy sweep through their hearts.

*So are you telling me I should publish this?* Yes. Humanity needs to allow the seeds to germinate before the full exposure traumatizes a lot of beings. If they never think outside their beliefs from childhood and conditioning, when this church falls they will not understand and not want to believe they were fooled. They will blame it on the work of "the devil" because they have been conditioned to believe everything they were told is truth. And most have never even tried to go within for their own truths. Some beings are just not able to question their beliefs because they are either young souls or just too traumatized. This is about beings with an actual soul. This will also create a lot of anger.

With additional information now, some beings will hear the truth in their hearts. They are awakening en mass and have the ability *to feel* the truth. In general, people have a way of hanging on to their beliefs so tightly and we are trying to help as many as possible loosen their grips and awaken to truths they might not have thought about prior. When everything changes in your ordinary reality and people see the truth of the connection with non-ordinary reality they might be better able to think outside the box they have been in for so long without as much fear.

*I have many more questions but I think that is enough for now. Thank you for all of this. You gave us plenty to think about. This is so much more than I thought I would be writing about. I felt your nudge earlier and knew STRONGLY I needed to write about dream travels. I didn't think I was going to write about my dream specifically.*

I AM always here for you.

For my readers I would like to add that if this doesn't resonate with you, no worries. If you were triggered at all by the content please just give it time to sink in without judging it. We are all entitled to our perspectives, right? This was shown to me on November 4, 2018 for reference. We can all have our perspectives and continue cleaning up this planet together as we all go through these very interesting times together. I personally believe all is being revealed and will continue to surprise people at incredible speeds as the dominoes fall - especially over the next period of time.

# CAN WE STOP HURTING EACH OTHER

◆ ◆ ◆

There is a growing trend in the spiritual communities to discredit people. It was easy to spread among those just waking up: people who are searching for answers, people who have questions and people who are reaching out in desperate need of assistance. All it took was for a few questions to be raised, judgmental as they may have been, *for fear and doubt to take on it's own thought form of darkness.*

**I'm talking about notions of who *may or may not be* false leaders of light.**

The rumors started with statements like: *"If they actually **say** they're a healer then they must not be - a true healer would never self-identify themselves."* Or this:

*"A true Master or teacher would never call themselves that."* etc.

Those who are not healers, teachers or master healers have no way of understanding what those who are, have gone through. And a lot of us have just remained silent about it. Myself included.

**But it continues and it's hurting newly awakened people. So I'm breaking my silence.**

I pose this question for your consideration: When someone goes to medical school and pays thousands of dollars for their education, training and experience, do you tell them they should not identify themselves as such? Or a therapist. Or a Chiropractor...

How about this question: If someone just starts to wake up and they're looking for a Reiki practitioner who is at the Master level (because perhaps they are thinking about training in Reiki), are you saying the Reiki Master should not identify as such? How would anyone be able to find such healers then?

Don't you think it's kinda of ridiculous to say that someone who has spent time and money to learn a trade, profession or career shouldn't advertise or identify their specialty or level of expertise?

***Of course that's ridiculous!***

The establishment uses initials after names to show levels of credentials and it's a sign of prestige and honor.

*There is one big, screamingly obvious difference in this argument I would like to point out.*

If a person goes through the establishment for their career, meaning college, it is often assumed when they get their Masters or Doctorate degree they are competent and capable of establishing a practice where they often charge quite a lot of money. Not all do, but it is somewhat expected.

However, when a person chooses to train as a healer they are doing what their spirit is guiding them to do. A lot of them have to keep regular jobs because clients don't often have enough money to pay for services that would enable the healer, teacher or practitioner to run a full time business. Insurance doesn't pay for Healers.

Most often healers don't follow this calling for money. It's more of a ***service-to-humanity-thing.***

When they reach a certain point that I liken to a crisis, they have a choice to go ALL IN and try to make a living doing what they know they are here to do.

They are following their inner guidance and *they are being of service to humanity and the planet.*

This witch hunt and crowd gang mentality must stop.

If you think about it for just a few minutes you can see that *no person in their reasonable mind,* (without being brainwashed or conditioned by others) *would expect healers to* ***not*** *identify themselves.*

Many have been on a very dark and lonely path. It hasn't been easy trying to break down these old constructs and help flip this planet being of service to others and still pay their bills.

Many have gone through a lot of years taking only small donations or not charging at all and questioning if they even *should charge* for their services - because they have beautiful bright souls who just want to share their gifts.

**But are you going to walk into your doctors office and say,** *"Hey Doc, you became a doctor so you could help people heal, right? I think you shouldn't actually* ***say*** *your a doctor. No doctor* ***who is a real doctor*** *would identify themselves. Therefore, you must be a false doctor."*

See the flawed logic? You can see how ridiculous

that sounds... *I hope.*

In any case I needed to get this short bit out because I listened to a rant yesterday on YouTube on one of my favorite channels. They had a list of things that should help people identify false light beings. And believe it or not, people who call themselves master healers or teachers was on the list... *I. Kid. You. Not.*

I'm not going to judge because that is exactly what I heard coming from others. Not just the person on the video acting like an expert in knowing who is real light and who is false light, but the commenters were bandwagon jumpers. There were some valid points of things to watch out for in this video but I still wasn't resonating with this person's overall content.

Listen, we are all here together and we all have to work this out together. If you are stuck in duality then you probably feel like you have to have an opinion on this for whatever reason. Perhaps your opinion has even changed about this topic.

**Staying in the Middle is Always Best**

I got triggered so I'm writing about my experience

hoping to *shed a little light from my vantage point.* I've been a Master Healer since 1998, so this is not just a recent experience for me.

I have a decent perspective and have a mostly clear view - *I was triggered, so not completely clear I suppose, lol* - But I've *been there* and I've *done that...* ***all of it.***

I paid my dues and I've given more sessions and trainings away than I can count. I've also dealt with the guilt of charging and I've dealt with learning how to honor myself and my gifts. And I never stop learning.

None of this has been a quick or easy path for any of us and it's never been about the money. I suspect most people who are healers at whatever level feel the same way - at least, most healers I have encountered over the years feel similar.

It is very important that we all learn how to use our own discernment and not get swayed by something someone else says. Try to use you critical thinking skills before you jump on any bandwagon that may be going down a dark road to harsh, cruel and unfair judgments of others.

It's also probably not a good idea to put everyone in a box just because they self-identify what they do based on their education; or identify themselves at a certain level of expertise which they have attained...***in any field***.

Energy work takes time, money and practice, just like any other profession. Try to remember to be kind and compassionate when making comments about all people in any particular field.

**What is right for you may not be right for someone else.**

If you really want to know if someone is (so-called) true or false, try this to remember: We all have both light and dark within. We're learning how to balance in the sacred neutral middle. Listen with your heart and if you don't resonate with someone's energy you simply know to move on. *Why* you don't resonate is not important. **Just move on.** Also, listen to their speech. The sound of someone's speech should give you a clue about whether or not you resonate with them.

That is how you can tell if someone is right for you to engage with, or not. Otherwise just leave them alone and let them be. There's a great saying, *"don't feed the trolls"* and people like that will also find their way - just like you will find your way.

This can obviously be applied to any area in your life. Take the micro lesson here of attacks in the healer community and apply it to any other area. If other people are judging, name calling, bashing, criticizing, on *any kind* of witch hunt or you hear gossip that's out of control, perhaps take a step back without jumping on any wagons and use your critical thinking skills.

There are always micro experiences in your personal life and macro level experiences for the collective. They say you must first clean your own house before you can clean your neighborhood.

**So can we all please stop throwing stones at each other?**

# MAKE YOURSELF HAPPY

## *Completing Yourself*

Over the last month or so, I've heard from a number of people who are struggling with relationships. Why struggle? If it isn't working out then why stay? Why do we try to force a relationship if it's bringing us so much pain? If there is a lesson to learn allow the learning process, (don't ignore it and keep cycling through the same thing) thank the pain for teaching you and then move on without feeling the need to stay in a relationship that is continually causing pain.

We all know relationships are sticky business when it comes to fighting, pain and residual battle scars. It also seems so simple to just say, *'walk away'*. Most of us know it's not that simple to just walk away from certain relationships, especially ones that we have built our lives around or with the expectation of doing so.

I will tell you right up front in full disclosure and full honesty that I do not consider myself an expert romantic relationship advice-giver. With that being said, I can tell you without a doubt what has most definitely not worked in my life and from my spiritual perspective, why this was the case.

**If you see male and female as strictly opposites and gender based only, therein lies a problem.**

Most people understand the concept of opposing but complementary forces such as yin and yang, um and yang, night and light and so on. When one is learning about such concepts it is typical to also see male and female lumped into the equation. This could be confusing serving to only reinforce constructs that enforce separation with inequality at the root.

However if you are speaking as male and female energies that are opposing but complementary forces and with the eventual merge concept, then there is no problem and you must grasp this concept well.

I challenge you to see further. I challenge you to see beyond the typical descriptions of what you've been conditioned to perceive in a limited and linear way. I challenge you to see the male and female both within yourself; for you truly have both energies as part of your unique energetic signature.

Think of your energetic signature as your unique blueprint. An energetic signature is to your spirit, as a thumbprint is to your physical body. Your energy is Universal Life Force which is androgynous as your rate of vibration increases - as your density lightens.

The beautiful part is that higher frequency energetic signatures are made up of both divine male and divine female whole and complete packages. The wholeness for which we've longed for in our relationships and the completeness for which we have been searching for our entire lives has been tucked away safely in our hearts all along.

**We Are Searching For Ourselves.**

We are on this journey to find ourselves and we never had to look any further than our own hearts. If we keep looking for someone else to complete us - or make us happy - and we keep looking on the outside for someone or something else to fill our void then we can never truly find the happiness for which we are seeking.

Our longing comes from an innate desire to finish our own personal completeness. When we unite the inner male and the inner female we become complete. We feel whole and our cup is then full. We don't need to take energy or steal it from others by trying to fix them (because we know better) or try to tell them what they should or shouldn't be doing (because we know better).

We know within our hearts that we have to do our own inner work to complete ourselves and this requires us to actually do the work, ourselves. There is no other way. You cannot pay someone else to do it for you and you cannot pay someone else to tell you what to do or magically remove and heal all your *stuff*.

**Only YOU can do this work for yourself!**

You can pay someone to remove blocks, read from your records, heal something, attune something, tell you about your 'past' lives or even connect with your deceased loved ones. They will probably have some good and generally loving messages for you too. There are many skilled ones here helping others. But times are changing. People are waking up to the fact that everyone has gifts and abilities. There is no exclusion to your birthrights. If you do the work you will reconnect to your Source.

When you start to trust your own inner power your internal guidance gets stronger - like a muscle - and with some discipline and practice you will be able to start navigating with your spirit in charge again. Your memory will come back online as you begin to trust the male and the female within you. Both have an equal half to your Divine wholeness.

If you are holding your light strong people come to your field and healing will occur naturally. I'm definitely not saying that you should or shouldn't go to see someone and pay them for their expertise. On the contrary. We need to discern the difference between when to ask for help and when we are just being lazy with entitlement drama.

**Self Empowerment Is The Key!**

There are people who can help get stagnant energy moving so you can remove issues for good. But when someone does energy work for you of any kind and gets it moving, unless you do the inner work and stop allowing old records to keep playing on broken mode, the issues will not completely resolve and will repeat until you fix yourselves. Remember that lessons are repeated until they are learned and denial is a very long river.

I know this sounds harsh for the newly awakened ones. I promise you this is not as it seems. When you make a decision to take full responsibility for everything in your life things start changing and your understanding grows to catch up to your wisdom. You cannot have access to wisdom you do not understand.

You must first decide with your intention to change and grow and then what happens is absolutely amazing... you change and you grow and you understand the wisdom that your heart is guarding very carefully, until you are ready.

**Your Mission Right Now Is To Complete Yourself**

Spiritually complete energetic signatures - with male and female combined - are able to bring transformed human consciousness into multidimensional planes of existence. The realms for which we visit during dream time (only to often forget our nightly travels) will become the reality for which you soon discover is the true baseline of your existence.

You remember to live every moment finding joy in anything and everything. When there seems to be no joy around you, it is then that you choose to remain neutral and do not get sucked into the drama all around. You plant your seeds of light by just shining it. You do not hide. You share what you have because your cup is full not because you are told that makes you a good person. You choose interaction or no action, versus reaction. Remember wisdom is knowing whether or not to say something.

You become the living example for everyone around you and all those who come into your field just because this is your Universe. Everyone has the ability to create and live in their very own Universe centered and grounded within their human hearts.

As you ascend, find the joy in as many moments as you choose to let your heart smile. When your heart smiles the light is recognized by all other lights; just as your darkness is also recognized. Choose to take your personal responsibility, stop blaming and complaining and do the inner work. You are ascending whether you are consciously aware and awake or not.

# TREASURES FROM THE PAST

## *Revelations From My 24-Year-Old Self*

I recently rearranged my furniture as I often do when I feel certain shifts in energy and my space needs to reflect these changes. This most recent act of '*feng shui'ing*' or better stated '*going with the flow*' and clearing, revealed a small file cabinet that I've avoided going through.

When I moved in May 2017 it seemed easier to just place some pretty material over the black piece and use it as a corner table - since I thought it only contained old paperwork and other items I needed to purge during a future rainy or snowy day.

After this particular shift I felt a strong urge to get to it and I'm glad I listened. My blog would have to wait. YouTube would have to wait. Netflix would have to wait. I began going through the files one by one and was surprised that it wasn't that long ago I had indeed purged the paperwork and what remained was not as old or as cluttered as I thought.

Obviously it didn't take nearly as long as I expected. So I decided to clean out the two top drawers as well. I found an old hand-held tape recorder and about a half dozen micro cassette tapes. Immediately I tried to play them and with only two new AA batteries and a few bangs of my hand, it worked!

**Divine Timing is Always on Time!**

I'm finding such joy in being pleasantly surprised when I see Divine Timing unfold in special ways, such as these cassette tapes speaking to me from the past. Much to my delight I was listening to my younger 22, 23 and 24 year old self - over those 6 cassettes. I also observed as both the speaker and the listener - my current operating system was coming from the roots of my 5D system.

There was absolutely no self-judgments, only reflections, love and gratitude for all the experiences, especially the ones with harsh struggles and deep pain. Particularly, the deep-rooted pain of not belonging here that I could feel down to my core back then. An attempt to take my own life at the age of 21 resulted from the complete and utter dispair and isolation I felt of being so misunderstood and lonely. Which I now understand, many can relate.

Although I remembered exactly how emotionally painful life can be - triggered by my own words - when I listened with my entire being I only felt a deep love and appreciation for myself and my chosen path. That was one of the times I reincarnated within my own body, which is a topic for another time.

It has all served me well and my perspective was refreshed with waves of joy and gratitude. I suppose one could say the emotional pain and residual scars have finally been healed.

My first husband and I purchased that hand-held recorder when I finally got diagnosed with third-stage Lymes disease. I was getting instructions from a nurse about self-administering the IV medications I would be taking for some months and my husband wanted to make sure to get it recorded.

I could hear how young I sounded, I remembered how scared I was. I also remembered how horrible I felt battling these physical symptoms with no diagnoses for several years and barely any support from the medical community until I finally got a diagnosis.

Lymes disease just started hitting mainstream in the early nineties and I apparently had one of the more chronic and long-term cases since it went so long without being properely diagnosed and treated. The details of that entire experience can be shared another time. But it's good to shed and transform that entire experience now that I understand better why this was my chosen path.

On these cassette tapes I also listened to myself going through my first divorce and the beginning stages of self empowerment. I had a therapist named Kate F. who helped me so much. She taught me about self respect by helping me to learn and understand I was allowed (and encouraged) to set healthy boundaries. That was a very big lesson for me as I was also an unaware empath at the time. She was the first person who taught me it was ok to say no to other people. I am so grateful for her guidance during that time in my life.

**Out Of My Own Lips**

I heard myself talking to this little recorder as if I was speaking to my future self I did not know yet. I was saying things I needed to do (or work on) or do more of... even though I didn't realize this was exactly what I was doing *(speaking to my future self)* or that one day I would listen to myself with such joy and happiness for all that has come to pass, including the pain and hardships.

I was saying that I needed to stop caring so much about what other people think about me. I heard myself saying that I was proud of myself when I set a boundary and didn't bend. I was enjoying the process of blooming after I realized I was indeed much stronger than I had been told by forces that no longer could control me.

**I was allowing myself the gift of self respect and the birth of my own self empowerment.**

I started a journey to conscious self respect and claiming my self empowerment. I didn't always get it right and often had to repeat lessons until they were learned. I like to call it *falling forward.* I am so grateful for all those experiences.

How else could I ever teach empowerment until I had truly learned it for myself? It has taken me years since to mature in that self empowerment after 24 years of listening to a broken record inside my head while struggling to following my heart through all the conditioning, expectations and rules of social norms imposed on most people from the time they are born, myself included.

Ultimately I still chose those conditions. I believe I chose them in order to break free from them.

Balancing karma and balancing yourself is a journey, as is healing ancestral karma. If you could go back in time and talk to your younger self *what would you say*? Do you keep journals? Did you record yourself? What if you could go forward to speak to your future self, would you want to tell them anything? Consider writing yourself a letter, seal it and tuck it away.

If someone had told me when I was 24 that I could and would be speaking to my future self when I made those recordings I would not have believed them. However, this is exactly what happened and it wasn't any kind of supernatural time-travel event - and yet, that's exactly what it felt like.

But the time-bending direct experience came from a micro cassette recorder long since forgotten. I heard my 24 year old self speak to me on a multitude of levels and our hearts are one at the center of it all. How beautiful is that?

My younger self got to speak very clearly to me! She

told me she was ready for the journey. She may not have known what was ahead but she was willing to get back up, dust herself off and keep going. She had courage even through her fear of the unknown and she was willing to keep following her heart - as she so often did.

I could not have felt more love for her as I did that night. The circle of life felt complete - at least with these particular life experiences. It was similar to closing a book not just turning to a new chapter.

# SOUND SENSITIVES

*Now is the time for all good men to come to the aid of their country*

I have typed that one sentence more than any other sentence in my life. I was around nine or ten and just starting to show interest in typing. My dad told me if I practiced that sentence over and over, my speed would increase and I would get very good at typing.

Needless to say, I typed it over and over in hopes of getting better.

It was true my errors decreased and my speed greatly increased. In fact, I had ideas running wild through my young head that if there ever was an Olympic event for typing I might just bring home to the gold! My memories of typing practice are fond ones and I did enjoy it very much. It also gave me a chance to be alone and I greeatly valued my alone time even as a young child.

When I actually dig into what was so appealing, I know the sounds of the clicking typewriter was one major reason that drew me in so much. I found the sounds the typewriter made to be incredibly soothing. Perhaps because my dad was a court reporter and I had often heard these sounds when he worked from home. Since he worked at the office a lot in my younger years, I enjoyed when he was at peace working from home.

**Sounds By Association**

What was it about the sounds the individual keys made all playing together in concert that made me feel so relaxed? Was it the way the subtle clicking of the individual keys sounded (and my physical response to it) that seemed to have no particular rhythm and yet always blended in such a fascinating way?

Perhaps there was also something yet to be identified, discovered and eventually named. I was born in 1969 so during my childhood - and most of my adult life - there was no name for what I could actually feel in my body with sounds.

Additionally, it's not a secret that we often find familiar sounds that gave us comfort as a child to also be comforting as an adult. But I discovered another reason. At least for me, this makes a lot more sense.

**Sounds Can Physically Feel Good**

Sounds are literally vibrations and just as vibrations can put you in a bad mood, they can also uplift your energy and put you in a good mood. I'll be focusing on the good feels because this is my choice of focus. Sounds and vibrations can also do so much more but that is for another time.

Anyone can train themselves to be sound sensitive.

I realize that is a big statement and there's also a general opinion that some people simply just can't 'get the tingles' or they are somehow immune to the effects of ASMR for example. If you've never heard of ASMR, let me first give a brief explanation.

Autonomous Sensory Meridian Response (ASMR) is defined in Wikipedia as:

*"A term used for an experience characterized by a static-like or tingling sensation on the skin that typically begins on the scalp and moves down the back of the neck*

*and upper spine. ASMR signifies the subjective experience of 'low-grade euphoria' characterized by a combination of positive feelings and a distinct static-like tingling sensation on the skin."*

In my humble opinion this 'definition' barely scratches the surface.

**Learning the Language of Sensation**

Personally, I get physical sensations all over my body and have for as long as I can remember. Sometimes I would describe them as just 'the chills' but as I got more in tune with myself I discovered my body was actually talking to me.

Learning how to interpret which signals meant what has been *(and still is)* a learning process. When I listen to my body I learn faster and when I don't listen it's like my body is speaking a foreign language.

Every person on this planet has the capability to develop this communication skill. But just like anything, practice is necessary for self-mastery. It will always be a learning *process* so if choose to learn it, get used to it and you'll fall in love with the process.

If you have ears and skin and you can hear and

feel, you can also feel the sensations from ASMR. Whether or not you need a little practice is another thing. Sounds can trigger feelings of relaxation and anyone is capable of feeling these responses.

**Can Everyone Feel?**

Of course everyone can feel. Then why do some people claim they don't get the physical responses from typical triggers? Simple: *there's a disconnect between the body and the mind.*

**No problem!**

If you want to feel the physical sensations of an ASMR trigger or become more sound sensitive and listen to the language of your body, put your ear plugs or headphones on, go to YouTube and search for a facilitator who's voice or whisper you like. If you don't like any voices, there are plenty of videos that do '*No Voice*' or '*No Talking*' content.

More importantly, allowing yourself the time to relax and unwind is a key factor. If you have too much stress in your life and you're unable to connect to your body, that is a major sign that you need to slow down and give yourself the gift of YOU.

## Acceptance and Receiving

Time to relax and unwind can be done in so many ways but allowing yourself to receive this time is also honoring yourself. You are literally saying to the Universe that you're willing to receive. Perhaps meditation is also not easy for you. Most people who say *that* are those who are unable to connect with their body as well.

It's most important that you learn and practice how to connect because then it becomes automatic and natural. You remember that you've always known how to do it and the pleasant joy and peace that your body sends as communications to you becomes one of the cooler things you can experience in a body.

Have I always been sound sensitive?

It would appear so and as I recall various times when sounds would trigger pleasant physical sensations, I can say for certain that a lot of my sensitivities were apparent even before I attuned to Reiki Healing; but also significantly increased and began to make much more sense in my early twenties and then moreso after learning energy healing.

Since everyone is different nobody has the same path for when you open, unlock and begin recognizing your gifts. Therefore it's also extremely important that you stop comparing yourself to other people saying when you should or shouldn't connect. When your time is right you will find your way. Trust that.

**My advice for anyone looking to feel more pleasant sensations and make a direct connection using their body for signals and open communications is this:**

1) Surround yourself with uplifting sounds.

2) Listen to music that brings you joy and happiness.

3) Invest in some decent ear plugs or headphones and use them with YouTube content designed to help you relax (ASMR, Meditation or Hypnosis material).

4) Make time everyday to give yourself inner-time (ie meditation or quiet contemplation time) and find your connection to this amazing biochemical suit you call a body.

5) Get good at identifying sounds that help you and sounds that don't - remove as much of the negative sounds and vibrations as you can and increase the former. This includes removing people from your life whose speech seems to bother you for no apparent reason - trust that there is a reason and you are

clearly not resonating at a rate of vibration that's in synch with your highest good.

It's very true that people project frequencies from their voice (in addition to other methods). If you're learning about how you do and don't resonate with people and curious why you may feel that somone's voice just bothers or relaxes you, this could help your understanding better. We are attracted to and repelled by *(just like a magnet)* energies everywhere and all the time. Vocal tone is no exception. I hope this helps you begin to find your personal connection between your body and mind and get things rolling.

# ASCENSION IS ONGOING

*Ignorance Is Not An Excuse Anymore*

The ascension is occurring everywhere. Whether this is the first time you've heard about it or if you've been on the path for some time, you are experiencing this process because you chose to be here when you volunteered pre-birth to be in a human body - remember or not - and you were granted this incredible opportunity.

As we continue down the path of awakening there are many blogs, websites and videos that share ascension stories complete with the signs, symptoms and synchronicities that go along with awakening. As I have watched, listened to, and read about different types of people's experiences, I recall various experiences of my own throughout my life.

My awakening was a little slower and more spread out over many years in contrast to those who chose a much quicker wake-up path during this time period. There were several important junction points or '*dates with destiny*' that helped trigger a more comprehensive experience allowing me to fully understand I was receiving transmissions, healings, upgrades and downloads.

A lot of those experiences seem to have occurred while I was by myself physically but I know I was never alone. Expecting some big shifts to occur while attending group events never seemed to happen as expected or anticipated.

The hype of opening and connecting that was implied or flat-out promised in promotional literature for any such workshop or event was still very convincing and did provide me with enough to keep me curious and questioning everything, learning from many, many different sources. When you're on the path and hungry you will not stop actively learning by choice.

**My Body, My Brain... I Choose My Belief Systems**

I never felt right about someone else telling me what to believe or what to have faith in; or what to trust or not to trust. To me that seemed like the ultimate form of brainwashing. Someone else creating a belief system for you is in fact, a form of brainwashing. I much prefer to have free will over my own belief structures, how my brain works and thinks as-well-as my own life choices, *thank you very much.* I will decide what I believe in or if I want to suspend my belief systems until I have more information.

Since everything is fluid and subject to change, why wouldn't my beliefs change as well? If I am so stuck in even my core beliefs and I'm unwilling or unable to allow for them to evolve then I am only hurting myself remaining in a state where I am unwilling or unable to grow. Stagnation is never comfortable.

I choose growth. Personally speaking, that is the best choice I can make for myself. If I don't choose growth then I remain stubborn in not allowing new information to flow and come to light. If I believe in something that turns out to be a lie then why wouldn't I change my mind and adjust that particular belief system? Seems quite silly to remain in those old beliefs, doesn't it?

◆ ◆ ◆

## Disclosure Is Happening Even If You Don't Believe It

The problem we are facing at this time is that corruption is being exposed and people are learning some ugly truths they would rather not hear. If you are not hearing these disclosures then you are either: 1) *not listening*, or... you are: 2) *still stuck watching - and believing - mainstream TV news programs* that are classified properly as 'ENTERTAINMENT'. If this is news to you (pun intended) and you feel you may be stuck in either category, I highly suggest you dig in and *DYOR immediately. There is more than enough information out there for you to sink your teeth into. (*DYOR = Do Your Own Research)

**The Train's Leaving the Station!**

We are in the midst of much disclosure occurring on this planet. Those who are so rigid in their beliefs seem to be unwilling or unable to suspend beliefs (or disbeliefs) and are having quite a difficult time while grasping for the old systems that have been shoved upon them from their birth in human bodies. And yet, they can feel something is wrong and they may be missing the boat.

Some people do still tend to think that if they ignore some of these disclosures that *'it'* will simply disappear, perhaps also thinking things will *go back* to the way they used to be at the height of ignorance.

This is most definitely not the case. A quarter in America has 'heads' as a label for one side and 'tails' as a label for the other side. Both are opposing but yet, complimentary sides of the same coin. The point a lot of people seem to miss is that the quarter is still 25 cents no matter which *'side you choose'*. The total value of both sides of the whole coin is much better than if you were to try and cut off the other side, or kill off, or quiet down, or prove wrong, or whatever... This analogy can obviously be applied to any**thing** stuck in duality where you have two opposite sides to anything, really.

Hence why the middle ground is always welcome for a terrific view of all sides but truly only valuable when both sides are combined and working together, in unity. Opposing but complimentary forces within every single person on this planet is no different. You have the divine masculine and the divine feminine energies within everyone and they need to combine in order for you to become a whole and complete being.

Truth will always come out and it is already setting people free, but you can never go backwards on this journey. Denial is similar to a festering disease. Denial will eat away at you shaming you into feeling so bad about yourself for not feeling worthy enough to know the truth. When you actually hear it, you may be so numb to discernment and so disconnected from your highest self that allowing the truth to be felt - instead of just heard - will just not seem possible.

**It Is Always Possible To Reconnect**

Triggering people to respond with denial was an ongoing effort. This was the dirty plan that has been running your conditioning. You can change that plan. You can use your free will and decide to get on the train because it's leaving the station. DYOR

You can choose to stay in ignorance or you can free yourself. Truth can be offered but only you can make that decision. One of our greatest gifts is free will and it's only valuable if we choose to actually use it.

You will find the more you learn on your ascension journey inward the more you need to learn. This can be celebrated. It is only when you decide to feed your ego/personality that you stop learning, which will always trick you into thinking you know it all.

You may feel you are older and have accumulated enough knowledge that you know best, or at least better than most people. Perhaps you do. However, if you are rigid in your beliefs that you held as a child then you are still just a child, spiritually speaking.

Moving beyond your conditioning and allowing your third dimensional cup to be emptied while accepting that there is so much more you don't know, will allow your heart to expand and the keys to your inner connection to become known. Just remember that how you choose to move forward will become apparent to other awakened ones around you.

Are you living a truly authentic life? Are you following what you are told you *should* do? Are you following your passions? Rather, are you passionate about what you are doing in life? Does your work make you happy? Are you helping others with your gifts? Do you even know what your gifts are? Have you met your true inner self yet? Are you even searching for your true self? Do you know where you came from? Are you searching for answers about why you are here on this planet?

Do these questions make you feel uncomfortable? It's ok to feel uncomfortable because that is how you know where you need some work, some inner work. As long as you are in a physical body you are supposed to feel, everything. People used to actually ignore and tuck away their feelings, imagine that. It's because of fear.

If you are still looking out into the world to blame, criticize and rationalize everything that doesn't fit into your personal belief structures about why things should or shouldn't be done a certain way (according to you and your beliefs), then it's certainly time to take that light you claim you have and shine it back in on yourself.

You are shining a light out into the world and expecting to see reasons for why things happen but those reasons are nothing more than a corrupted filter or a twisted lense that you are viewing your reality from - that is your perspective. There is nothing wrong with it per say, it is yours.

Everyone is entitled to their own perspectives and opinions. It is only when you try to layer and project those beliefs onto other people where trouble happens. This has been the case for a very, very long time.

When we truly desire to live in peace and harmony that we can respect every single diversity and every single path that each individual of the entire whole is entitled to live for their personal experiences (for whatever reason), that we can then begin to see choices for what they are and without judgements.

We are here to experience, grow, learn and play. This is a game called life and our inner child wants to be let out of time-out now.

*~ The time has come for all inner children to be allowed back out to play again ~*

If you benefitted from these teachings and would like to learn more, I provide free content on my YouTube channel, Lynda Light.

Made in the USA
Middletown, DE
10 July 2021